This Bible Verse
Coloring Book Belongs To

_____

_____

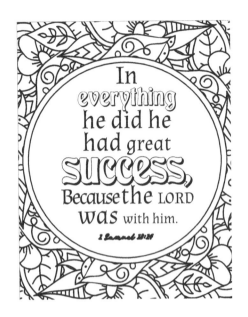

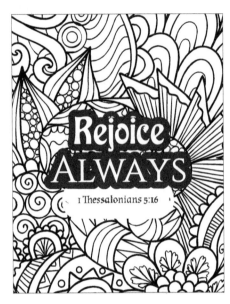
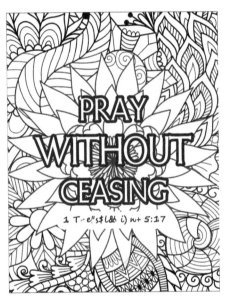

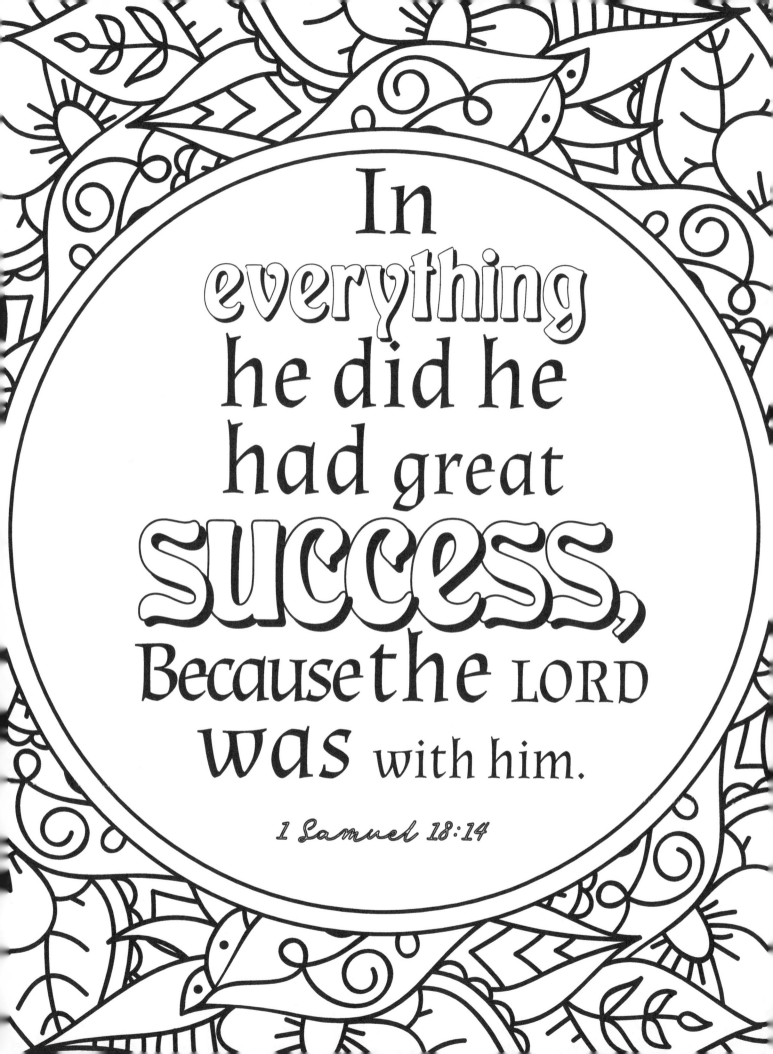

For this is the love of God, that we keep His COMMANDMENTS. And His COMMANDMENTS are not BURDENSOME.

1 John 5:3

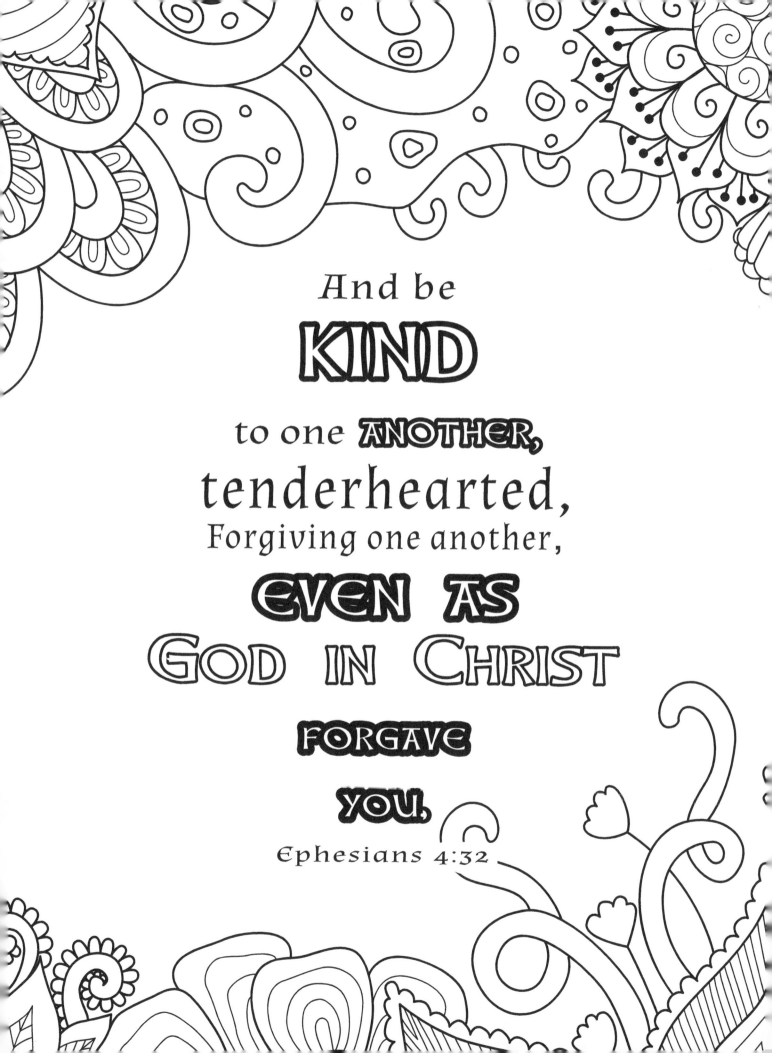

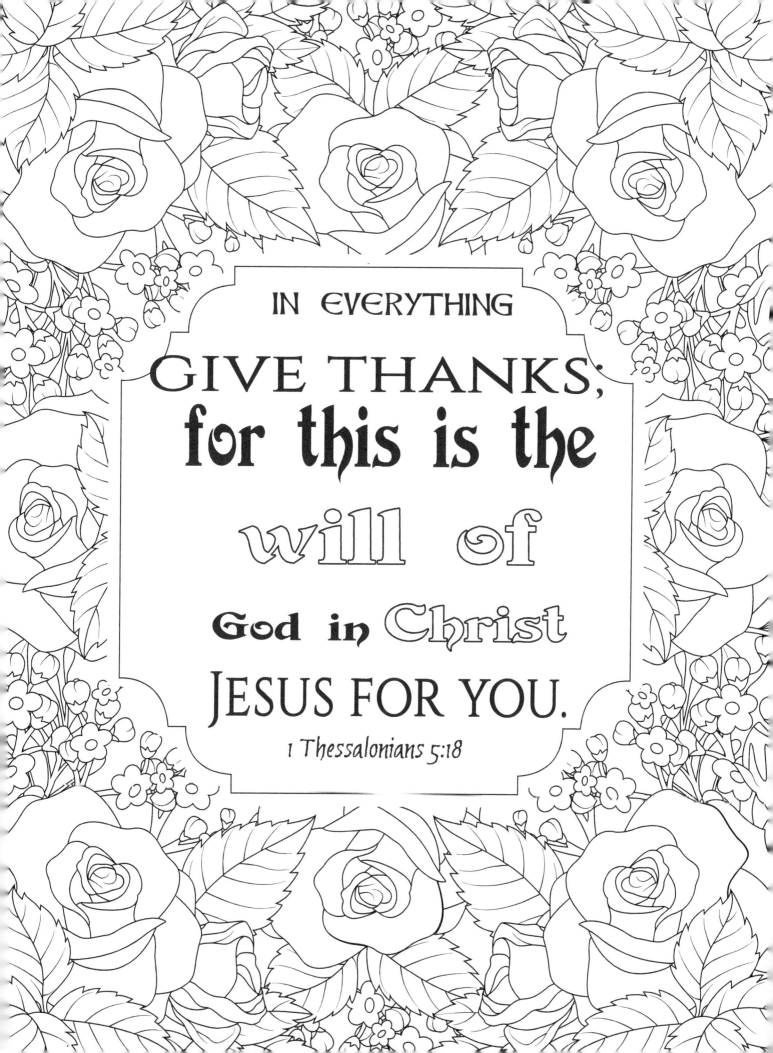

So keep the words of this covenant to do them, that you may prosper in all that you do.

Deuteronomy 29:9

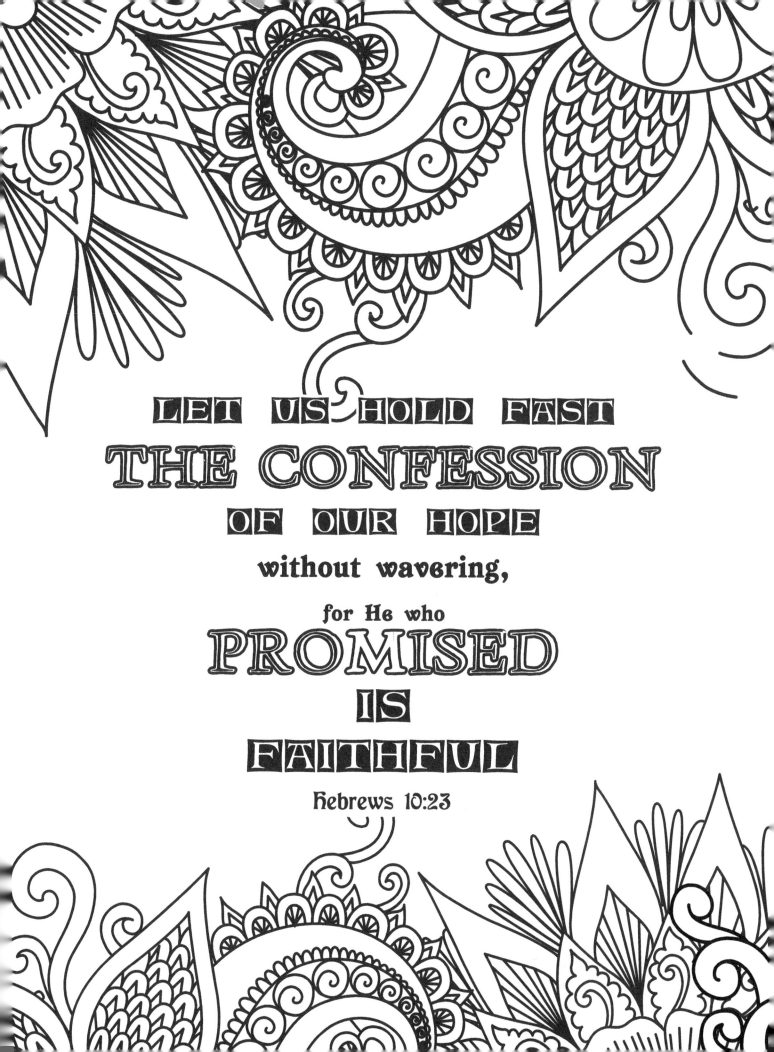

Without counsel, plans go awry, But in the multitude of counselors they are established.

Proverbs 15:22

Let the *words*
of my mouth
and the *meditation*
of my heart
Be *acceptable*
in **Your Sight**

Psalm 19:14

Delight yourself also in the Lord, And He shall give you the desires of your heart.
Psalm 37:4

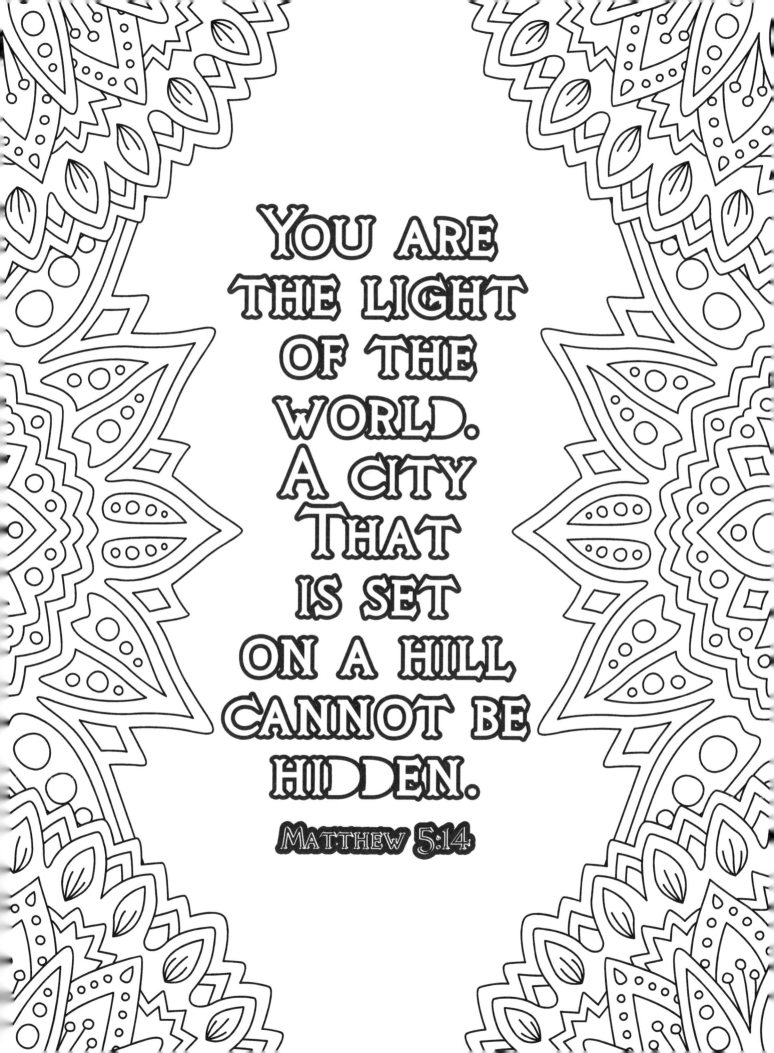

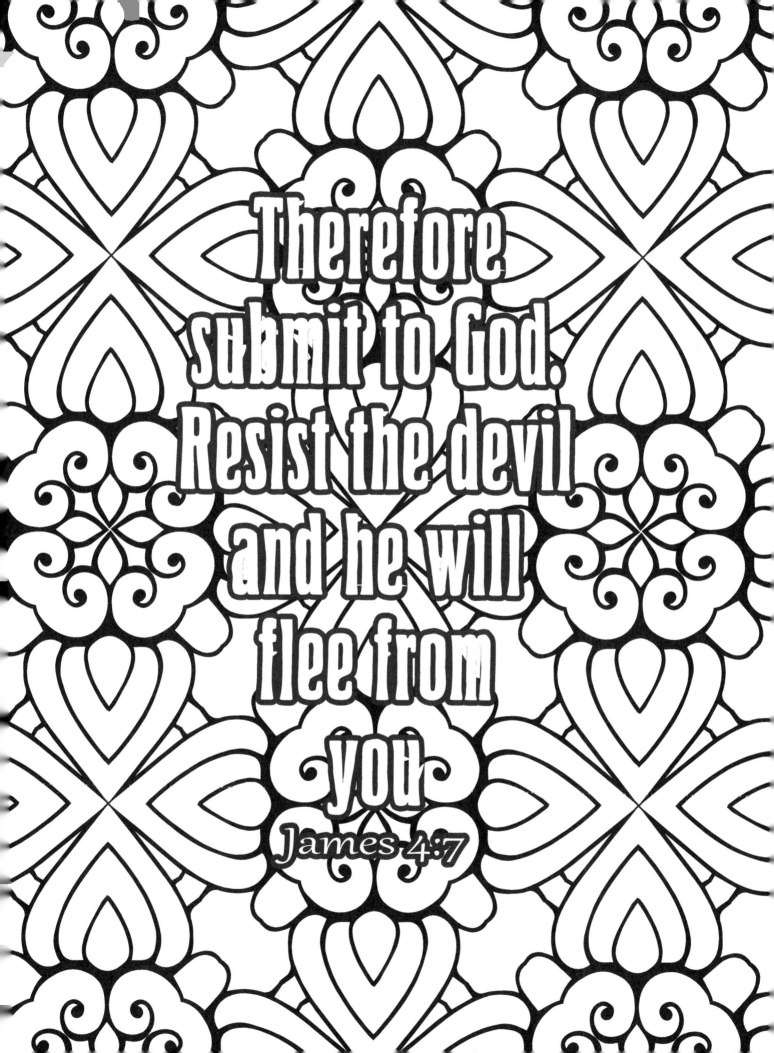

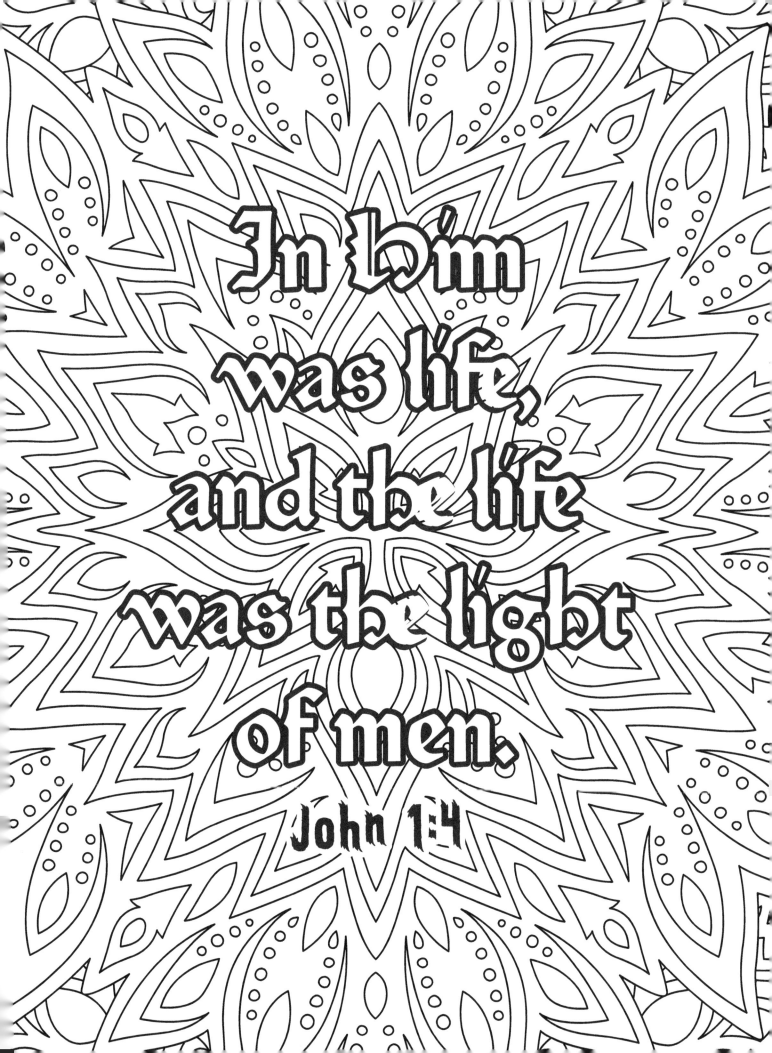

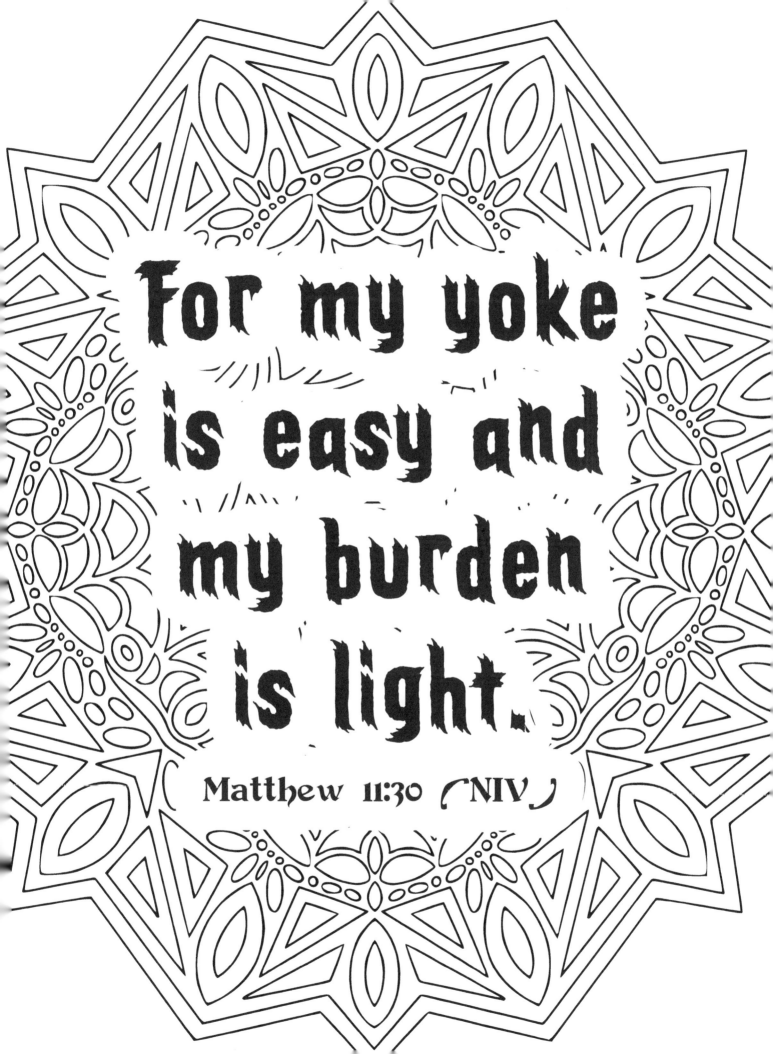

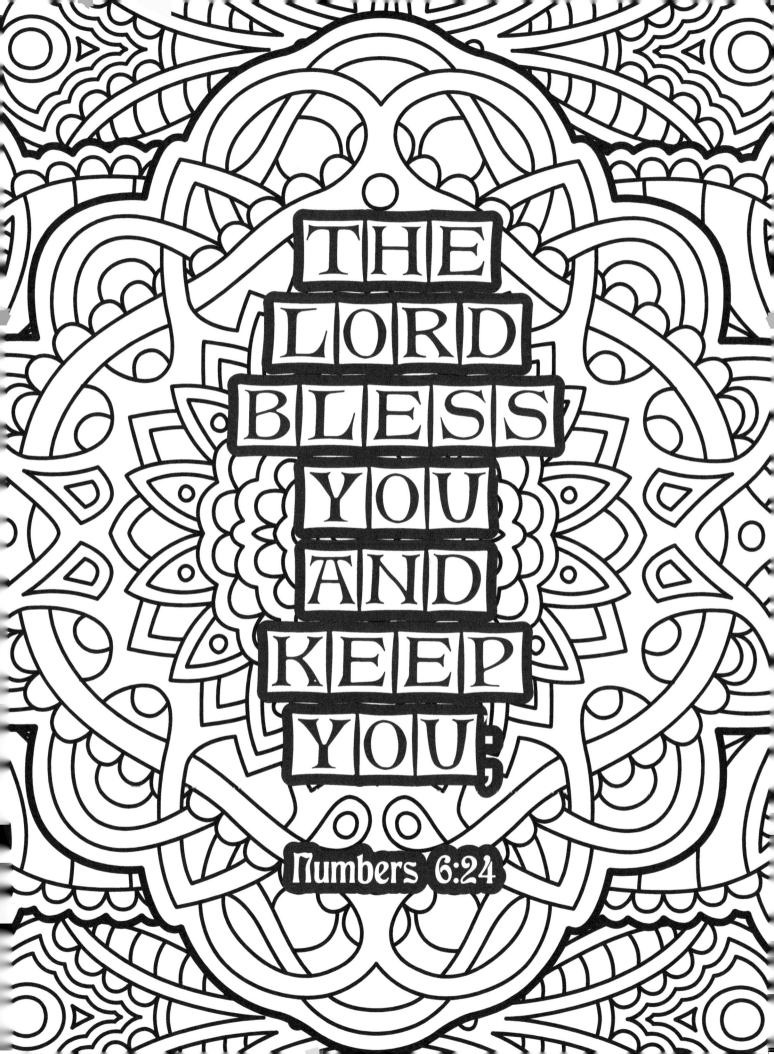

The name of the Lord
is a strong tower;
The righteous run to it
and are safe

Proverbs 18:10

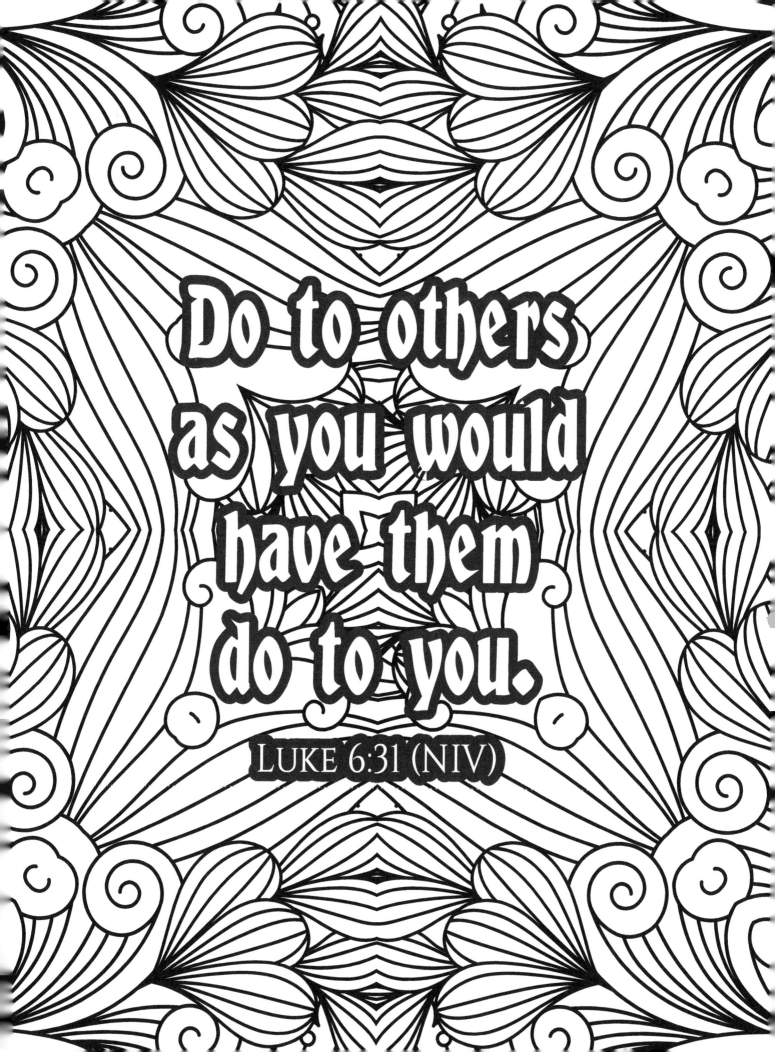

Oh, give thanks to the *Lord*, for He is *good*! For His mercy endures *forever*.

Psalm 136:1

Commit your way to the Lord,
Trust also in Him,
And He shall bring it to pass.

Psalm 37:5

REJOICING IN HOPE,
PATIENT IN TRIBULATION,
CONTINUING STEADFASTLY
IN PRAYER

Romans 12:12

THE LORD IS GOOD TO ALL,
AND HIS TENDER
MERCIES ARE OVER
ALL HIS WORKS.

PSALM 145:9

The Lord is my light and my salvation, whom shall I fear?

PSALM 27:1

This is the day
the Lord has made;
We will rejoice and be glad in it.

Psalm 118:24

I have hidden your word in my heart that I might not sin against you.

Psalm 119:11

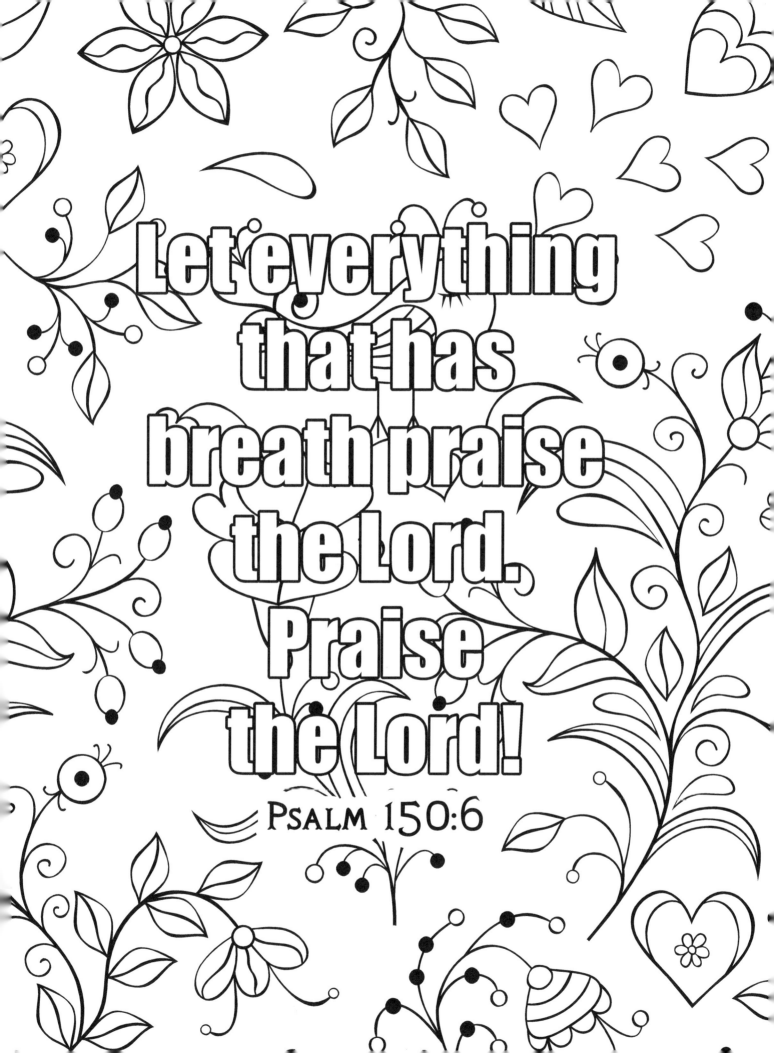